Easy 4 me 2 Learn
Speed Writing

The 21st Century alternative to Shorthand
International/American spelling version

A training course with easy exercises to
learn faster writing in just 6 hours with the
innovative BakerWrite™ system and internet links.

Heather Baker

www.UoLearn.com

Easy 4 Me 2 Learn™

Speed Writing the 21ˢᵗ century alternative to Shorthand. International/American English spelling version

A training course with easy exercises for faster writing in just 6 hours with the innovative BakerWrite™ system and internet links.

Published by: Universe of Learning Ltd, reg number 6485477, Lancashire, UK
www.UoLearn.com, support@UoLearn.com

ISBN 978-1-84937-012-7

Other editions:
ebook pdf format 978-1-84937-018-9
ebook epub format 978-1-84937-010-3
Other imprints: Speed Writing Skills Training Course 978-1-84937-011-0
British English spelling 978-1-84937-003-5

Easy 4 me 2 Learn, Universe of Learning and UoLearn are trademarks of Universe of Learning Ltd.

BakerWrite is a trademark of Baker Thompson Associates Ltd and is used with permission.

Illustrations by Corne-Enroc, Buenos Aires, Argentina, www.Corne.com.ar
Proof reading by Rita Mistry.
Edited by Dr Margaret Greenhall.

The publisher and author assume no liability for any loss or damage, personal or otherwise which is directly or indirectly caused by the application of any of the contents of this book.

Contents

About the author

Heather had over twenty years' experience as a secretary and PA before setting up Baker Thompson Associates Limited in 2000. The company specializes in the training and development of secretarial and administrative staff, www.bakerthompsonassoc.co.uk.

She now travels all over the UK working with large and small companies to enable their office staff and PAs to work more effectively and efficiently. She also delivers courses in the Middle and Far East. Heather is a Certified NLP Practitioner.

She worked for ICI Pharmaceuticals (now AstraZeneca) and Hewlett Packard; she spent 5 years in France working for the Commercial Director of Cognac Hine and then 10 years with Granada Media working up to Personal Assistant to the Managing Director, commuting regularly between their offices in Manchester and London.

She developed this speed writing system to fulfil a requirement by many companies for a quick and easy way for their employees to take notes. The course became very popular and she was often asked if there was a book with the basics of the system – so here it is!

Heather has been married to Ian since 1979 and they have two daughters, Ailsa and Erin. This book is dedicated to them with profound thanks for all their support over the years.

Have Fun!

How did BakerWrite come into being?

When I was asked to teach speed writing (but not shorthand), I investigated various systems. All of those I researched seemed to have the same basics, which I also use; silent letters, omitting vowels, phonetic options, etc.. However, it was the more advanced issues of prefixes and suffixes which seemed to me to be too complex.

I thought about the two shorthand systems with which I am familiar – Pitman and Teeline – and realized that I could use some of the techniques they employ, but still using letters. That is where the idea came from for the subscript and superscript.

I also thought that many people may feel restricted by rigid systems and so wanted to ensure that learners could feel they were able to adapt the method to suit their preferences. I offer guidelines rather than principles, suggestions rather than rules.

Best Wishes

Heather

Praise for Heather and the BakerWrite system of speed writing

✓ "This was the best course I have ever attended."
  "I learnt a lot and will be able to put it into practise straightaway."

✓ "The principles are very easy to follow, and I am already using it to take notes."

✓ "BakerWrite is the easiest shorthand system I have come across. Having studied all the major shorthand systems and even other speed writing courses, I find BakerWrite a sheer delight."

✓ "I feel that BakerWrite could be a complete shorthand system."
  Robbie, Glasgow

✓ "Your system is so easy to learn and use."
  Dawn, London

✓ "I like the way the book is easy to carry around and it's so simple to understand." *Sue, Manchester*

✓ "The best things about this event were the enthusiasm of the teacher, the fact it was interactive and the helpful information. It was an excellent course; clear, concise and really enjoyable and I would recommend it to others. This course could not be improved, it was brill!"
  University of Salford

✓ "The speed writing trainer was informative, relaxed and helpful. Excellent. She was very helpful, enthusiastic and approachable. She made the topic more fun and less scary. All the examples really helped and brought it to life."
  The Jockey Club

- ✓ "The tutor was excellent – a thoroughly enjoyable day."
  The Jockey Club

- ✓ "I will recommend this course to everyone who takes notes."

- ✓ "Excellent course, well delivered – lots learned."

- ✓ "I thoroughly enjoyed the course."

- ✓ "My expectations were exceeded with this course."

- ✓ "Heather you are very helpful and supportive – excellent course."

- ✓ "Trainer was very helpful, friendly and informative and also very encouraging."

- ✓ "Heather had a way of relaxing/de-stressing all which enabled people to keep going and take it all in."

- ✓ "Tutor was very helpful and able to answer all questions. It was good having the person who invented the system to do the course."

- ✓ "Heather was patient and was more than able to answer our questions."

- ✓ "Heather is very friendly and the course was presented in an easy to understand way and at a good pace."

- ✓ "I liked the trainer's straightforward way of explaining the subject matter with the practical sessions."

- ✓ "Heather took the necessary time to answer questions and to ensure the group was happy and comfortable."

- ✓ "I will use this system all the time."

- ✓ "Used daily this system could have a major impact."

- ✓ "The training was exceptionally well delivered. Heather was extremely helpful, patient and good humored, even when being tested by some of the group!!"

- ✓ "A wonderful day – thank you v much."

How to use this book

The bad news: You might be having difficulty keeping pace when you take notes at the moment.

The good news: you will be able to learn how to write much faster when taking notes.

The bad news: You need to do the exercises and to practice.

The final good news: The book is laid out as six easy to follow, guided hours, with lots of exercises.

All the answers to the exercises are at the back of the book, along with a dictionary.

To make it even more fun, we've got two pals who are going to help you throughout the book - Norbuz and his little friend Spikybuz.

If there are new words they'll be pointing, if you've got work to do they will be writing.

If you need help then can email us via www.UoLearn.com authors section where you'll find a link for Heather.

Now, the exercises in the book come with spaces to write, if it's your own book we invite you to do this. If you can't or it's a library book, we have a free downloadable workbook and dictionary in the 'Speed Writing' section of the website.

When you are making fast notes it is often from someone speaking so we've got some recorded extra exercises on the website too. Special thanks are given to Ailsa Baker for providing the voice for the dictations. There is one for each chapter and they are found on the website, www.Uolearn.com.

First hour

Silent letters and vowels

"Learning is a treasure that will follow its owner everywhere." Chinese Proverb

First hour:
Silent letters and vowels

In the first hour you will learn the basics of BakerWrite and you will have an opportunity to think about the abbreviations you already use when you are texting or taking notes quickly.

You will get some tips on how to practice BakerWrite to enable you to remember the abbreviations, and some tips on technique.

The basics:

Things you probably already use:

Abbreviation	Meaning
&	and
c	see, sea
i	I
r	are
u	you
y	why
2	two, to, too
4	four, for, fore
no	number
nb	note well
ie	that is
etc	and so on
eg	for example

Let's add to that:

Abbreviation	Meaning
s	is
t	it
f	of
b	be, being, been
m	me
w	we
v	very
hv	have
th	the*

*You could also use a full stop instead of th for the and then use / for the end of a sentence.

Notes:

For very common words like 'of' we drop the initial vowel.

Where there is more than one meaning (e.g. b = be, being or been) then the context will make it clear which you want.

Also symbols:

=	equals
?	question, why
+	plus
<	less than
>	more than
∴	therefore

And you probably have many more of your own.

In order to learn a new system of speed writing (or shorthand) it is vital to practice regularly and, unfortunately, only constant repetition will work.

You know how you learn all the jingles and products from the TV adverts because they are broadcast so often.

> ### Exercise 1 : What abbreviations do you use?
> Here's a blank table, add a few of your abbreviations to it.

Abbreviation	Meaning

Top tips for practicing:

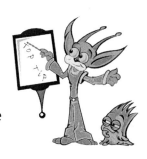

- ✓ At the end of each section of theory (as above) write the speed writing outline about 10 times while saying the word in your head (don't repeat the longhand – you know that!).

- ✓ Then dictate the words to a partner or put them onto a tape recorder and play them back to take them as dictation. This is important as it replicates the work situation. You need to be able to react quickly when you hear a word to build up speed.

- ✓ Reading is OK sometimes, but it is important to build up your ability to hear the word and write it quickly; you won't do this by reading only.

- ✓ Always write the words across the page, not down, as you would if you were taking notes.

- ✓ When you're drilling new groups of words, keep reminding yourself of words you drilled earlier.

- ✓ Don't copy from the book. Look at the abbreviation once and then write it from memory.

- ✓ Always use lower case – capital letters really slow you down. Use handwriting rather than printing, unless you usually print. This system is intended to make your life easier, not more difficult! If you find a particular combination of letters difficult to write, often you may write that combination in another word – think how you join them there (for example, some people find writing ltl for little a bit awkward; see how you write l and t in the words bolt or halt).

- ✓ Also make your writing small and close together and don't press too hard with your pen or pencil – you will become very tired.

- ✓ You should use acronyms wherever possible (e.g. nhs, bbc).

With that in mind, I must reiterate that these are only guidelines not rules; if there is some part of the system you don't like, then don't use it, but do find an alternative that suits you. As long as it creates a shorter version of the word or phrase then it should be fine.

So have a go first of all at drilling the list of abbreviations from above.

Space for you to practice:

Silent letters:

> *Omit all silent letters – just write what you hear.*

A good example of this of this is 'i c u' for I see you.

Abbreviation	Meaning
no	know
tl	tell, till
scs	success
btr	better
ltl	little
cf	cough

Notes:

In 'know' we don't pronounce the k or the w and we'll talk more about vowels next.

With words like till and tell remember the context will make it clear when you are writing in sentences.

Words can be written phonetically too, like cough.

Exercise 2 : Drill the words then speed write:
1. I see the butter.
2. We have success.
3. I have very little.

COMMON WORDS

And remember some other familiar abbreviations:

Abbreviation	Meaning
mbr	member
dpt	department
org	organized organization
mtg	meeting
mkt	market

Here are some ways to differentiate between common, similar words:

tn	than
tht	that
thr	their, there, they're
thm	them
thn	then
ths	these
thy	they
thi	this
thos	those
wr	were
wh	what
whn	when
whr	where
whl	while
wl	will
wi	with
w/in	within
w/ou	without

Vowels:

> *Leave out vowels unless you need
> them to clarify your meaning.*

Abbreviation	Meaning
md	mad
sl	sell, sill
bt	bet
fl	fill
clr	collar
bg	bug

> *Also for clarity you could include just long vowels, i.e. you
> don't have a vowel for sell
> or fill but you do for seal or file.*

mad (md)	made
bet	beat
sel	seal
fil	file
col	coal
bugl	bugle
vlu	value

Exercise 3 : Drill the words then speed write:

1. The file is full.
2. We know the value of the file.
3. I sell at the market.

Exercise 4 : What would you use for the following words?

Abbreviation	Meaning
	hello
	dear
	yours
	please
	feel
	try
	book
	address

You may also want to include vowels (long or short) if you feel there may be some ambiguity of meaning. Often the context makes it clear what your abbreviated word means, but occasionally it may not be obvious; we will look at this later.

You may also occasionally want to add other letters for clarity. We use "no" for no, know, number and November; if you feel you may get confused you could use "no" for no and know, "num" or "#" for number and "nov" for November.

> *However, having suggested you miss out vowels wherever possible, there is one place you should always use them, and that is at the beginning of a word.*

If I were to write "nspr" I would probably assume the word begins with an n. In fact I wanted to write inspire. If I write "inspr" it is immediately clear what the word is.
Some other words to drill:

Abbreviation	Meaning
if	if
efct	effect
afct	affect
acpt	accept

> However, where a word begins ex you don't need to include the e as that clearly should be there:

xtnsv	extensive
xmpl	example
xcpt	except

Exercise 5 : Drill the words then do the sentences below:

1. I have an extensive effect on the class.
2. It is mad to work for other people.
3. Organization is the key to success.

> ### Exercise 6 : First hour summary exercises

1. Do you accept my view is better?
2. I bet you beat the eggs.
3. Please accept this free sample.
4. You know he sells files.
5. The department had success.
6. It is better to seal the file.
7. The value of the meeting is better.
8. Go to the market for value.
9. Except for me, the group knows you.
10. A little success is very good.

1 ....
2 ....
3 ....
4 ....
5 ....
6 ....
7 ....
8 ....
9 ....
10 ....

Once you've finished each hour remember to visit
www.UoLearn.com where you'll find an audio exercise.

You'll also find free copies of all the exercises as a printable
workbook and a copy of the dictionary.

Second hour
Phonetics and prefixes

"I didn't have time to write a short letter, so I wrote a long one instead." Mark Twain

Second hour:
Phonetics and prefixes

In the second hour we continue with further options. Some of these are definitely not obligatory. They involve some phonetic options – that is when words look like they sound, rather than how they are written.

We also introduce the use of subscript characters. This means we drop a character below the line to represent a commonly used group of letters.

You will get some tips on preparing for note-taking situations.

We then move on to prefixes. Prefixes are common beginnings to words. For these we use superscript characters; this means we raise a character above the word (like using quotation marks) to represent common prefixes.

Phonetic options:

> *Some people like to use more phonetic ways of writing.*
> *If you do then you may like to try these examples,*
> *if not just use the usual letters.*

> *Use a k for the letter k and also for a hard c:*

Abbreviation	Meaning
k (cn)	can
kd (cd)	could
kas (cas or cs)	case
klnk (clnc)	clinic

The non-phonetic version is in brackets.

> *However, you should always use a k to replace ck:*

bk	back
lk	lock

> *For a soft c, continue to use c:*

ces	cease
cntr	center

> You could also use a j for the letter j and for soft g:

Abbreviation	Meaning
aj (ag)	age
mnj (mng)	manage
jj (jg)	judge*
klj (clg)	college

*In words like judge we don't really pronounce the d.

> Some other ways of reducing your writing is by using 2 letters instead of 3 for abbreviations for months and days:

ja	January
fe	February
ma	March
ap	April
my	May
ju	June
jl	July
au	August
se	September
oc	October
no	November
de	December
mo	Monday
tu	Tuesday
we	Wednesday
th	Thursday
fr	Friday
sa	Saturday
su	Sunday

Exercise 7 : Drill all the new words, then try this:

1. I can carry the case back to the center.
2. Can you manage to get the judge to the college?

Exercise 8 : What would you use for the following words?

Abbreviation	Meaning
	hedge
	tick
	track
	clear
	desk
	link
	candle
	second
	crisp
	cell
	lucky
	piece
	fudge

Next we are going to introduce the use of subscript and superscript.

> *First of all we are going to use a subscript c $_{(c)}$ to represent the letters ch or tch:*

Abbreviation	Meaning
e_c	each
t_c	touch
te_c	teach
$_c k$	check
f_c	fetch
w_c	watch or which

Your brain tells you that you can't do this as for many years you have always written a c on the line – keep practicing, it will become easier.

> *If you want to abbreviate even more, you could also use subscript t $_{(t)}$ for th, and s $_{(s)}$ for sh. etc,*

c_s	cash
$_s wr$	shower
$_t nk$	think
$o_t r$	other

Again, this is optional.

Exercise 9 : Drill those words and then try the dictation.
It may feel strange at first but you will get used to it.

1. Pay for the book.
2. Give me a check for the bill.
3. The book is big.
4. Can I see the bell?
5. Can I have the value of the new book?

Top tips:

✓ When you are going to take notes in meetings or dictation, it is always a good idea to have practiced your abbreviations as much as possible beforehand. One of the reasons people can't read back their notes is because they make up abbreviations during meetings and then can't remember what they meant.

✓ If you've prepared in advance you will know what to write and what your abbreviation means. You can add to the dictionary at the end of the book or download a printable copy from www.UoLearn.com.

✓ Think also about people's initials, departments in your organization, products and/or services.
How could you abbreviate these? When you have finished this book, you will have all the knowledge you need to start making up your own abbreviations. More of this later....

Prefixes:

We're now going to look at some examples of prefixes.
A prefix is found at the beginning of a word and the
abbreviations we will use are for the very common prefixes.

> *We're going to use a superscript c [(c)]*
> *for the prefixes con and com:*

Abbreviation	Meaning
[(c)]sdr	consider
[(c)]pr	compare
[(c)]plx	complex
[(c)]mty	community
[(c)]tmpry	contemporary
[(c)]slt	consult
[(c)]tct	contact
[(c)]plint	compliant
[(c)]plant	complaint

> *Use a superscript d [(d)] for des and dis:*

[(d)]pr	despair
[(d)]ma	dismay
[(d)]apr	disappear
[(d)]aprv	disapprove
[(d)]prv	disprove

Exercise 10 : Drill those words and then do this exercise:

1. I despair of you.
2. We contact the clinic.
3. Could you consider the effect.

Space for you to practice:

Exercise 11 : Second hour summary exercises

1. The community considers each case.
2. I was dismayed at the lack of success.
3. The other check was lost.
4. Consult the judge each day.
5. He disappeared to teach the class.
6. Did you consider each complaint?
7. Can you manage to compare the centers?
8. I fetched the watch back from the clinic.
9. Could you cease, please.
10. How much cash do you have?

1 ....
2 ....
3 ....
4 ....
5 ....
6 ....
7 ....
8 ....
9 ....
10 ....

Remember to go to www.UoLearn.com for your hour 2 dictation exercise and downloadable workbook.

Third hour
More prefixes

"Our greatest weakness lies in giving up.
The most certain way to succeed is always to
try just one more time." Thomas Edison

Third hour: More prefixes

In this hour we continue with some more examples of superscript characters being used for common prefixes.

Use a superscript f $^{(f)}$ or a 4 for the prefix for and fore:

Abbreviation		Meaning
^{f}tl	4tl	foretell
^{f}cst	4cst	forecast
^{f}wrn	4wrn	forewarn
^{f}nm	4nm	forename

Top tip:

✓ Be very careful to make the f clearly superscript, otherwise it will just look like a capital letter and may confuse you. Also, decide which version you prefer and stick to that. If you keep changing this could make your transcriptions more difficult.

Use a superscript i $^{(i)}$ for inter and intro:

^{i}m	interim
^{i}rpt	interrupt
^{i}dc	introduce
^{i}vw	interview
^{i}nt	internet

Top tip:

✓ If you prefer not to dot the i that will speed things up too.

Exercise 12 : When you have drilled those new words, have a go at the following sentences:

1. Introduce me to the judge.
2. We could foretell the extensive damage.
3. We interrupt the meeting to check the lock.

Use a superscript p $^{(p)}$ for pro, per, pre:

Abbreviation	Meaning
^{p}pr	prepare
^{p}fct	perfect
^{p}mt	permit
^{p}vd	provide
^{p}psl	proposal
^{p}tct	protect
^{p}mot	promote
^{p}dct	product

Use a superscript s $^{(s)}$ for sub, sup or super:

^{s}mt	submit
^{s}prs	suppress
^{s}mkt	supermarket
^{s}prt	support

Exercise 13 : Practice the new words, then try this:

1. We provide the supermarket at the center.
2. The success of this project may compare well.
3. The supermarket sells big books.

Exercise 14 : What would you use for these words?

Abbreviation	Meaning
	fortune
	prefer
	programme
	introvert
	interfere
	supervise
	substitute

Space for you to practice:

Exercise 15 : Third hour summary exercises

1. Your forename is on the internet.
2. The forecast for the company is excellent.
3. Their interim figures are prepared and in the proposal.
4. Which supermarket do you visit?
5. I submit my proposal for the interview.
6. She interrupts me when I am at my desk.
7. Are you prepared to provide good value?
8. He protects his child from harm.
9. The product is introduced by the manager.
10. Consult the interim paper as soon as possible.

1 ....
2 ....
3 ....
4 ....
5 ....
6 ....
7 ....
8 ....
9 ....
10 ....

Your free hour 3 audio exercise is waiting for you at
www.UoLearn.com.

Fourth hour
Extra prefix ideas

"There is no happiness except in the realization
that we have accomplished something."
Henry Ford

Fourth hour: Extra prefixes

In this hour we will finish the prefixes.

Use a superscript t $^{(t)}$ for trans:	
Abbreviation	**Meaning**
^{t}prt	transport
^{t}fr	transfer
^{t}mt	transmit

Use a superscript u $^{(u)}$ for under:	
^{u}nth	underneath
^{u}stnd	understand
^{u}	under

Use a superscript m $^{(m)}$ for multi:	
^{m}stry	multi-story
^{m}pl	multiple

You will see that we have not used all the alphabet. That is because this system is very flexible and you can adapt it to your needs. You may prefer to use m for mega or any other prefix that would help you.

You could use two letters for longer prefixes, for example, ^{ac} for accomm or ^{rc} for recomm. ^{pp} could be used for propor.

In the NHS people use ^{a} for audio, ^{h} and $_{h}$ for hyper and hypo.

Have a think about what would help you. However, don't worry too much about words for which you already have abbreviations – stick with these; this system is meant to help you, not confuse you!

Exercise 16 : Some final dictation on prefixes to try, when you have drilled the latest group of words:

1. He tells me the transport is in the multi-story car park.

2. Do you understand the transfer must be made to provide the funds?

Exercise 17 : Fourth hour summary exercises

1. Please transmit the letters by email.
2. I understand you provide an excellent service.
3. The transfer was underneath the minimum amount.
4. Complaints have been received each week.
5. Multi-media is new this century.
6. The internet transmits data immediately.
7. He translates the documents from Spanish into English.
8. Do not underestimate the Chief Executive.
9. We recommend the member pays his fees.
10. It is not easy to accommodate students.

1 ....
2 ....
3 ....
4 ....
5 ....
6 ....
7 ....
8 ....
9 ....
10 ....

Have a look on the website (www.UoLearn.com) for the hour 4 exercise.

Fifth hour

Suffixes

"Nobody can go back and start a new beginning, but anyone can start today and make a new ending."
Maria Robinson

Fifth hour: Suffixes

Now we start to look at suffixes. Suffixes are common endings to words and, as for the prefixes, we will use a superscript character to represent a group of letters that make up some of the common suffixes.

*We're going to use the superscript b $^{(b)}$
for the suffixes ible and able:*

Abbreviation	Meaning
t^b	table
ps^b	possible
acs^b	accessible
avl^b	available
$rspn^b$	responsible
^{b}	able

and we can use prefixes and suffixes to **really** save time

$^c sdr^b$	considerable
$^c frt^b$	comfortable
$^p b^{by}$	probably, probability

Use a superscript f $^{(f)}$ for the suffix ful:	
Abbreviation	Meaning
hlp^f	helpful
jy^f	joyful
scs^{fy}	successfully

Use superscript g $^{(g)}$ for ing:	
wrk^g	working
shp^g	shopping
vst^g	visiting
dr^g	during
d^g	doing

You may not always just drop vowels; sometimes using the first 2 or 3 letters of a word can give a better clue :

inc^g	including
org^g	organizing
dev^g	developing

> *Use superscript s $^{(s)}$ for cial/sial/tial:*

Abbreviation	Meaning
so^s	social
rsdn^s	residential
ptn^s	potential
sp^s	special
spa^s	spatial*
spst	specialist

*Spatial is an example of where it is useful to put in the long vowel.

> **Exercise 18 :** Practice the new words, then try this:
>
> 1. The teaching has the potential to affect all students.
> 2. Our specialist services extend during the day.

Exercise 19 : Some words using the ideas in the fourth and fifth hours.

Abbreviation	Meaning
	transaction
	transform
	underestimate
	multicultural
	incredible
	permissible
	connectable
	cheerful
	mixing
	commercial

Space for you to practice:

Exercise 20 : Fifth hour summary exercises

1. The new employee has great potential.
2. Is it possible to provide specialist tables?
3. Her social skills are lacking.
4. The successful meeting lasted two hours.
5. During the interview he considered her replies.
6. In all probability, it will be working by Friday.
7. Are you available for organizing the department?
8. She is doing all she can to make people comfortable.
9. Accessibility is important to this company.
10. Your work has increased considerably.

1 ....

2 ....

3 ....

4 ....

5 ....

6 ....

7 ....

8 ....

9 ....

10 ....

Have a go now at the dictation for hour 5 at www.UoLearn.com.

Sixth hour

More suffixes

"The key is not in spending time but in investing it."
Stephen Covey

Sixth hour: More suffixes

Use superscript m $^{(m)}$ for ment:

Abbreviation	Meaning
pa^m	payment
invl^m	involvement
^{c}mt^m	commitment
dev^m	development
env^m	environment
dtr^{ml}	detrimental
fnd^{my}	fundamentally

Use superscript c $^{(c)}$ for nce:

s^c	since
^{c}fr^c	conference

Use superscript p $^{(p)}$ for ship:

ldr^p	leadership
mbr^p	membership
rla^{np}	relationship

Use superscript n $^{(n)}$ for sion/tion/cean:

Abbreviation	Meaning
sta^n	station
sta^{ny}	stationery
	stationary
m^n	mission
^{c}m^n	commission
^{c}ple^n	completion
edu^n	education
edu^{nl}	educational
o^n	ocean
^{i}n^{nl}	international
^{s}v^n	supervision

As with the prefixes, you can use any other letters for suffixes that are useful for you. You could use, in a medical environment, ^{i} for itis, or in education use ^{o} for ology.

One final tip, many words used in business are compound words, ie, one word made up of two words. For example, spreadsheet, broadband, lifestyle, portfolio. A good way to write these quickly is to use a / giving you s/s, b/b, l/s, p/f. Think of some examples in your working life.

Exercise 21 : Practice the new words, then try this:

1. My involvement in the expansion of the company was useful.
2. Any hardship will be taken into account.

Exercise 22 : Using the ideas from the sixth hour, what are your abbreviations for the following?

Abbreviation	Meaning
	contentment
	statement
	once
	ambulance
	existence
	fellowship
	connection
	foundation

Exercise 23 : What other syllables do you use frequently? Add to this table.

Abbreviation	Meaning
	ous
	ness
	anti/ante
	mis
	ivity
	less

Space for you to practice:

1. Transcription of speed writing is easy when you practice.
2. International supervision is vital to large companies.
3. It is fundamentally the hardship which causes problems.
4. Is your relationship with your team improving?
5. Their commitment is vital to the continuation of the business.
6. The organization's mission covers education and the environment.
7. Membership of this club is very difficult.
8. His involvement with the commission took up a lot of time.
9. Is her behavior detrimental to our department?
10. Our conference will be during the week.

1 ....
2 ....
3 ....
4 ....
5 ....
6 ....
7 ....
8 ....
9 ....
10 ....

Well done, your final exercise is at www.UoLearn.com.

Action plan

"I'm a great believer in luck and
I find the harder I work, the more I have of it."
Thomas Jefferson

Top tips:

You have now learnt the basics of BakerWrite but you need to continue to work on this skill to become adept. These are some thoughts that may help you.

✓ Get yourself an A-Z notebook and enter in it all the new words you have learnt so far or download the printable dictionary from www.UoLearn.com. This is a good way to revise the theory you've learnt and provides you with your own personalized BakerWrite dictionary.

✓ Next you should start to think about the words and phrases you need for your area of work and put these in your new dictionary with the BakerWrite equivalents.

✓ Start to introduce BakerWrite into your every day life, but start gradually. A good idea is to begin by using the ^{9} for ing then, after a couple of days introduce another prefix or suffix.

✓ Use more and more of the abbreviated words and symbols.

✓ Regularly go through the theory and drill any words that cause you problems.

✓ Get yourself informed. When you are going to take notes at a meeting or are expecting calls on a particular topic, anticipate what vocabulary you may need and work out the BakerWrite version for them, put them in your dictionary and drill them. In this way you will have a structure to work with.

✓ Visit either Heather's website www.bakerthompsonassoc.co.uk or the publisher's website www.UoLearn.com for any BakerWrite updates and to network with other users.

✓ Finally, don't put yourself under too much pressure. It does take time to become proficient so don't become stressed if you can't take notes quickly straightaway. However, do be tenacious. Don't give in – keep at it.

Gd Lk!

	My action plan:

Date	Action

Date	Action

Answers to the exercises

"I have to exercise in the morning before my brain figures out what I'm doing." Marsha Doble

Answers to the exercises:

These are suggested ways you could write the exercises. They aren't the only way and as you work with the BakerWrite speed writing system and you'll develop your own style.

Exercise 1 :

Your own choices.

Exercise 2 :

1. i c th btr.

2. w hv scs.

3. i hv v ltl.

Exercise 3 :

1. th fil s fl.

2. w no th vlu f th fil.

3. i sl @ th mkt.

Exercise 4 :

Abbreviation	Meaning
hlo	hello
dr	dear
yrs	yours
pls	please
fel	feel
try	try
bk	book
adrs	address

Exercise 5 :

1. i hv a xtnsv efct on th cls
2. t s md 2 wrk 4 othr ppl
3. org s th ky 2 scs.

Exercise 6 :

1. do u acpt my vw s btr?
2. i bt u bet th egs.
3. pls acpt thi fre smpl.
4. u no h sls fils.
5. th dpt hd scs.
6. t s btr 2 sel th fil.
7. th vlu f th mtg s btr.
8. go 2 th mkt 4 vlu.
9. xcpt 4 m, th grp nos u.
10. a ltl scs s v gd.

Exercise 7 :

1. i k kry th kas bk 2 th cntr
2. k u mnj 2 gt th jj 2 th klj?

Exercise 8 :

Abbreviation	Meaning
hj	hedge
tk	tick
trk	track
klr	clear
dsk	desk
lnk	link
kndl	candle
sknd (2nd)	second
krsp	crisp
cl	cell
lky	lucky
pec	piece
fj	fudge

Exercise 9 :

1. py 4 th bk.

2. gv m a $_c$k 4 th bl.

3. th bk s bg.

4. k i c th bl?

5. k i hv th vlu f th nw bk?

Exercise 10 :

1. i ^{d}pr f u.

2. w ^{c}tct th klnk.

3. kd u ^{c}sdr th efct.

Exercise 11 :

1. th ^{c}mnty ^{c}sdrs e$_c$ kas.

2. i ws ^{d}myd @ th lk f scs.

3. th o$_t$r $_c$k ws lst.

4. ^{c}slt th jj e$_c$ da.

5. h ^{d}aprd 2 te$_c$ th kls.

6. dd u ^{c}sdr e$_c$ ^{c}plant?

7. k u mnj 2 ^{c}pr th cntrs?

8. i f$_{cd}$ th w$_c$ bk frm th klnk.

9. kd u ces, pls.

10. hw m$_c$ c$_s$ do u hv?

Exercise 12 :

1. ^{i}dc m 2 th jj.

2. w kd ^{f}tl th xtnsv dmj.

3. w ^{i}rpt th mtg 2 $_c$k th lk.

Exercise 13 :

1. w ^{p}vd th ^{s}mkt @ th cntr.

2. th scs f thi ^{p}jct ma ^{c}pr wl.

3. th ^{s}mkt sls bg bks.

Exercise 14 :

Abbreviation	Meaning
ᶠtun (4tun)	fortune
ᵖfr	prefer
ᵖgrm	programme
ⁱvrt	introvert
ⁱfr	interfere
ˢvs	supervise
ˢstt	substitute

Exercise 15 :

1. yr ᶠnm s on th ⁱnt.

2. th ᶠcst 4 th co s xclnt.

3. thr ⁱm figs r ᵖprd & in th ᵖpsl.

4. w꜀ ˢmkt do u vst?

5. i ˢmt my ᵖpsl 4 th ⁱvw.

6. ₛe ⁱrpts m wn i am @ my dsk.

7. r u ᵖprd 2 ᵖvd gd vlu?

8. h ᵖtcts hs ꜀ld frm hrm.

9. th ᵖdct s ⁱdcd by th mnjr.

10. ꜀slt th ⁱm ppr asap.

Exercise 16 :

1. h tls m th ᵗprt s in th ᵐstry kp.

2. do u ᵘstnd th ᶠfr mst b md 2 ᵖvd th fnds?

Exercise 17 :

1. pls ^{t}mt th ltrs by eml.

2. i ^{u}stnd u ^{P}vd a xclnt srvc.

3. th ^{t}fr ws ^{u}nth th min amnt.

4. ^{c}plants hv b rcvd e$_c$ wk.

5. ^{m}med s nw thi cntry.

6. th ^{i}nt ^{t}mts data immed.

7. h ^{t}lts th docs frm spn$_s$ in2 engl$_s$.

8. do nt ^{u}est th ce.

9. w ^{rc}mnd th mbr pas hs fes.

10. t s nt esy 2 ^{ac}mdt stdnts.

Exercise 18 :

1. th t$_c$^{g} hs th ptn^s 2 afct al stdnts.

2. our spst srvcs xtnd dr^g th da.

Exercise 19 :

Abbreviation	Meaning
$^t ac^n$	transaction
^{tf}m	transform
$^u est$	underestimate
$^m cul$	multicultural
$incrd^b$	incredible
$^p ms^b$	permissible
$^c nct^b$	connectable
$_c r^f$	cheerful
mx^g	mixing
$^c mr^s$	commercial

Exercise 20 :

1. th nw emplye hs gr8 ptn^s.

2. s t ps^b 2 ^{p}vd spst t^{bs}?

3. hr so^s skls r lk^g.

4. th scs^f mtg lstd 2 hrs.

5. dr^g th ^{i}vw h ^{c}sdrd hr rplis.

6. in al ^{p}b^{by} t wl b wrk^g by fr.

7. r u avl^b 4 org^g th dpt?

8. $_s$e s d^g al $_s$e k 2 mk ppl ^{c}frt^b.

9. acs^{by} s imp 2 thi co.

10. yr wrk hs incrsd ^{c}sdr^{by}.

Exercise 21 :

1. my invl^m in th xpn^n f th co ws us^f.

2. ny hrd^p wl b tkn in2 acc.

Exercise 22 :

Abbreviation	Meaning
^{c}tnt^m	contentment
stt^m	statement
o^c	once
amb^c	ambulance
xst^c	existence
flw^p	fellowship
^{c}nct^n	connection
fnd^s	foundation

Exercise 23 :

Your own choices.

Exercise 24 :

1. ^{t}crp^n f s/w^g s esy wen u prctc.

2. ^{i}n^{nl} ^{s}v^n s vtl 2 lrj cos.

3. t s fnda^{my} th hrd^p w$_c$ css ^{p}blms.

4. s yr rla^{np} wi yr tem imprv^g?

5. thr ^{c}mt^m s vtl 2 th ^{c}tnu^n f th bus.

6. th org's m^n cvrs edu^n & th env^m.

7. mbr^p f thi clb s v dfclt.

8. hs invlv^m wi th ^{c}m^n tk up a lt f tm.

9. s hr bhvior dtri^{ml} 2 our dpt?

10. our ^{c}fr^c wl b dr^g th wk.

Space for you to practice:

Speed Writing
Dictionary

"Do not say a little in many words but a great deal in a few." Pythagorus

A	
able	b
accept	acpt
accessible	acs[b]
accommodate	[ac]mdt
account	acc
affect	afct
age	aj
all	al
amount	amnt
an	a
and	&
and so on	etc
any	ny
are	r
as soon as possible	asap
at	@
available	avl[b]

B	
back	bk
be	b
beat	bet
behavior	bhvr
bell	bl
bet	bt
better	btr
big	bg
bill	bl
book	bk
bug	bg
bugle	bugl
business	bus
butter	btr

C	
can	k / cn
carry	kry / cry
case	kas / cas
cash	c_s / k_s
causes	css /kss
cease	ces
center	cntr
century	cntry
check	$_c$k
child	$_c$ld
class	kls / cls
clinic	klnk
club	klb / clb
coal	kol / col
collar	klr / clr
college	klj/clg/clj
comfortable	^{c}frt^b
commission	^{c}m^n
commitment	^{c}mt^m
community	^{c}mty
company	co
compare	^{c}pr
complaint	^{c}plant
completion	^{c}ple^n
complex	^{c}plx
compliant	^{c}plint
conference	^{c}fr^c
consider	^{c}sdr

C	
considerable	^{c}sdr^b
consult	^{c}slt
contact	^{c}tct
contemporary	^{c}tmpry
continuation	^{c}tnu^n
cough	kf / cf
could	kd / cd
covers	kvrs/cvrs

D	
damage	dmj
data	dta
day	da
department	dpt
desk	dsk
despair	^{d}pr
detrimental	dtr^{ml}
development	dev^m
did	dd
difficult	dif
disappear	^{d}apr
disapprove	^{d}aprv
dismay	^{d}ma
disprove	^{d}prv
do	do
document	doc
doing	d^g
during	dr^g

E	
each	e$_c$
easy	esy
educational	edu^{nl}
effect	efct
email	eml
employee	emplye
English	engl$_s$
environment	env^m
equals	=
example	xmpl
excellent	xclnt
except	xcpt
expansion	xpn^n
extend	xtnd
extensive	xtnsv

F	
fees	fes
fetch	f_c
figures	fgrs/figs
file	fil
fill	fl
for	4
for example	eg
forecast	^{f}cst 4cast
forename	^{f}nm 4nm
foretell	^{f}tl 4tl
forewarn	^{f}wrn 4wrn
free	fre
full	fl
fundamentally	fnd^{my}
funds	fnds

G, H	
get	gt
give	gv
good	gd
great	gr8
greater than	>
group	grp
had	hd
hardship	hrd^p
harm	hrm
has	hs
have	hv
he	h
helpful	hlp^f
her	hr
his	hs
hours	hrs
how	hw

I	
I	i
if	if
immediately	immed
important	imp
improving	imprv[g]
including	inc[g]
increase	inc
inspire	inspr
interim	[i]m
international	[i]n[nl]
internet	[i]nt
interrupt	[i]rpt
interview	[i]vw
into	in2
introduce	[i]dc
involvement	invl[m]
is	s
it	t

J, K, L	
joyful	jy[f]
judge	jj
key	ke
know	no
knows	nos
lack	lk
lasted	lstd
leadership	ldr[p]
less than	<
letters	ltrs
little	ltl
lock	lk
lost	lst
lot	lt

M	
mad	md
made	mad
manage	mnj
manager	mnjr
market	mkt
me	m
media	mdia
meeting	mtg
member	mbr
membership	mbr^p
minimum	min
mission	m^n
much	m$_c$
multi-story	^{m}stry
must	mst
my	my

N, O	
new	nw
note well	nb
number	no
ocean	o^n
of	f
organization	org
organizing	org^g
other	o$_t$r
our	our

P	
paper	ppr
pay	pa
payment	pa^m
people	ppl
perfect	^{p}fct
permit	^{p}mt
please	pls
plus	+
possible	ps^b
potential	ptn^s
practice	prctc
practise	prcts
prepare	^{p}pr
probably	^{p}b^{by}
problems	^{p}blms
product	^{p}dct
project	^{p}jct
promote	^{p}mt
proposal	^{p}psl
protect	^{p}tct
provide	^{p}vd

Q, R, S	
question	?
received	rcvd
recommend	^{rc}mnd
relationship	rla^{np}
replies	rplis
residential	rsdn^s
responsible	rspn^b
sample	smpl
seal	sel
see	c
sell	sl
service	srvc
she	sh
shopping	shp^g/$_s$p^g
since	s^c
skills	skls
social	so^s
Spanish	spn$_s$
special	sp^s
specialist	spst

S	
speedwriting	s/w
station	sta^n
stationary	sta^{ny}
stationery	sta^{ny}
student	stdnt
submit	^{s}mt
success	scs
successfully	scs^{fy}
supermarket	^{s}mkt
supervision	^{s}v^n
support	^{s}prt
suppress	^{s}prs

T	
table	t^b
taken	tkn
teach	te$_c$
team	tem
tell	tl
than	tn
that	tht
that is	ie
the	th
them	thm
then	thn
there	thr
therefore	∴ /thr4
these	ths
they	thy
this	thi
those	thos
time	tim
to	2
took	tk
touch	t$_c$
transcription	^{t}crp^n
transfer	^{t}fr
translate	^{t}lat
transmit	^{t}mt
transport	^{t}prt

U, V	
under	u
underestimate	uest
underneath	unth
understand	ustnd
useful	usf
value	vlu
very	v
view	vw
visit	vst
visiting	vstg
vital	vtl

W, X, Y, Z	
watch	wc
we	w
week	wk
were	wr
what	wh
when	whn
where	whr
which	wc
while	whl
why	y
will	wl
with	wi
within	w/in
without	w/ou
work	wrk
working	wrkg
you	u

universe of Learning books

"The purpose of learning is growth, and our minds, unlike our bodies, can continue growing as we continue to live." Mortimer Adler

About the publishers

Universe of Learning Limited is a small publisher based in the UK with production in England and America. Our authors are all experienced trainers or teachers who have taught their skills for many years. We are actively seeking qualified authors and if you visit the authors section on www.UoLearn.com you can find out how to apply.

If you would like any of our current authors (including Heather Baker) to speak at your event please do visit their own websites (for Heather it's www.bakerthompsonassoc.co.uk) or email them through the author section of the UoLearn site.

If you want to purchase larger numbers of books then please do contact us (sales@UoLearn.com). We give discounts from 5 books upwards. For larger volumes we can also quote for changes to the cover to accommodate your company logo and to the interior to brand it for your company.

We have two main imprints – the Easy 4 me 2 Learn range (like this book) where the illustrations are fun cartoons and the Skills Training Course where the books are illustrated with photographs. For either imprint the aim is to take people through the development of skills by a range of exercises.

If you have any feedback about this book or other topics that you'd like to see us cover please do contact us at support@UoLearn.com.

Keep Learning!

Easy 4 me 2 Learn
Speed Reading

Triple your Reading Speed
On Screen and Paper

A training course with easy exercises for faster and effective reading on paper and computer.

ISBN: 978-1-84937-021-9, Order at www.UoLearn.com

Would you like to learn simple techniques to help you read 3 times as fast?

This book has a series of easy to follow guided exercises that help you change your reading habits to both read faster and to evaluate which parts to read and in what order.

Easy 4 me 2 Learn
Study Skills

How to Pass your Exams and
Course Work with Ease

Easy exercises to improve your learning skills for passing exams, memory training, note taking, essays and speed reading.

ISBN: 978-1-84937-020-2, Order at www.UoLearn.com

Study should be about extracting the information you need from the sources available as easily and quickly as possible. This book has a series of easy to follow exercises to help you become a super-learner.

Dr Greenhall's techniques helped her to get a first class honors degree in physics and chemistry, a doctorate in science and an MA in education, easily and with little effort. Guided exercises will help you to learn the secrets of these successes.

Coaching Skills Training Course

Your toolkit to coaching yourself and others, with exercises and scripts.

ISBN: 978-1-84937-019-6, Order at www.UoLearn.com

✓ An easy to follow 5 step model
✓ Exercises will help you enhance your skills
✓ Learn to both self-coach and coach others
✓ Work at your own pace to increase your ability
✓ Over 25 ready to use ideas
✓ How to use NLP in your coaching
✓ Goal setting tools to help achieve ambitions

A toolbox of ideas to help you become a great coach.

Increasing Your Influence,

A Guide to Developing the 7 Traits of Influential People

ISBN: 978-1-84937-022-6, from www.UoLearn.com

What are the characteristics that make some people more influential than others?

This book will give you the keys to successfully increase your influence at work and at home.

In this book you will discover how to:

✓ Decide what your influencing goals are and state them in a compelling way
✓ Find ways to increase your credibility rating
✓ Develop stronger and more trusting relationships
✓ Inspire others to follow your lead
✓ Become a more influential communicator

This book is packed with case studies, exercises and practical tips to help develop the traits required to become more influential.

CPSIA information can be obtained at www.ICGtesting.
Printed in the USA
LVOW101940251011

252043LV00003B/165/P